Stingy Kosiya
OF TOWN SAKKARA

©2015 All Rights Reserved

ISBN: 978-955-0614-77-6

Computer Typesetting by

Mahamevnawa Buddhist Monastery, Toronto
Markham, Ontario, Canada L6C 1P2
Telephone: 905-927-7117
www.mahamevnawa.ca

Published by

Mahamegha Publishers
Waduwawa, Yatigaloluwa, Polgahawela, Sri Lanka.
Telephone: +94 37 2053300 | 77 3216685
www.mahameghapublishers.com
mahameghapublishers@gmail.com

Stingy Kosiya
OF TOWN SAKKARA

*With the guidance and direction of
Most Venerable Kiribathgoda Gnānānanda Thera*

Artwork by Sumathipāla & Jothipāla

A Mahamegha Publication

Stingy Kosiya of Town Sakkara 01

My dear sons and daughters,

This is an entertaining story that teaches us about the unattractive trait of stinginess. During the time of our Gautama Supreme Buddha, there was a big town near the city of Rajagaha by the name "Sakkara." There lived a wealthy man of rank who owned a province worth 800 million gold coins. His name was Kosiya. But he was very miserly, therefore he was called

"Maccariya Kosiya," meaning Stingy Kosiya. He was so greedy he did not give even a minute part of his wealth to others, not even the equivalent of a dew drop on the point of a blade of grass. He neither spent his wealth on himself nor on his wife and children. Moreover, he did not give alms to virtuous and righteous people. His wealth was like a pond under the control of a demon.

Every morning, the Supreme Buddha attains the blissful concentration of Great Compassion (Maha Karuna Samāpatti) and survey the world to see who might need His help. That morning through that compassionate eye, the Supreme Buddha saw nobleman Kosiya. Even though he was stingy he had accrued great merit which could allow him to become a stream-entrant. Therefore, the Supreme Buddha compassionately thought of saving this man from rebirth in the four hells in his journey in samsara. The Supreme Buddha saw that it was the right time for Kosiya to realize the Dhamma.

That morning, nobleman Kosiya went to work for King Bimbisara. While he was returning from work, he saw a very poor man, who had been starving for days, greedily eating an oil cake. Nobleman Kosiya stopped and watched him carefully.

While the poor man was eating the oil cake, nobleman Kosiya's mouth started to water. He felt a strong urge to eat oil cakes.

Stingy Kosiya of Town Sakkara

"Oh, but how can I eat oil cakes? If I make them many others will gather around to eat them with me. Then I'll have to use up a lot of rice, ghee, honey, and oil. No! I cannot do that," said nobleman Kosiya. Then he left for the palace with his mouth still watering from the deep desire to eat oil cakes.

Just like a fire underneath the ash, the urge to eat oil cakes kept on resurfacing in Kosiya's mind. He kept on remembering how the poor man savoured the oil cake. Since he was constantly thinking about this, he became frail. His face became disagreeable. His body weakened. It became difficult for him to even breathe so he directly went to his bed and laid there, not speaking to anyone.

The nobleman's wife became very sad. She could not understand what had happened to her husband. She went to him and while stroking his head she spoke to him lovingly: "Oh, my dear husband, what has happened to you?"

"Nothing has happened to me" replied nobleman Kosiya.

"Why do you say that? You seem very different. You seem to be feeling rather sad. Your face and mouth have dried up. What happened? Did the King become angry with you?"

"No, no such thing happened."

"Then, did the children or servants offend you?"

"No, they didn't."

"Then, are you craving for something?"

At that, the nobleman went quiet. He did not give an answer.

Then, his wife said...

"Oh, my dear husband, if you're craving for something please tell me. I will try to fulfill your wish in every way I can."

Stingy Kosiya of Town Sakkara

Then, Kosiya looked at his wife with withered eyes. He became quiet for a moment and then told his wife…

"Yes…I…I do have a very strong …strong craving."

"Why don't tell me what it is, my dear."

"Oh, how can I tell you this?"

"Please, do tell me, dear."

Then, Kosiya hesitantly said…

"I have this deep urge in me. I am craving… I am craving for an oil cake."

The wife started laughing loudly.

"Oh, my dear, that is such a simple thing to satisfy. Are you a poor man? Let's make enough oil cakes for the entire town."

"What? For the entire town? Are you crazy? If they want to, they can make oil cakes and eat them themselves."

"Then my dear, shall we make enough oil cakes for those living in our street?"

"That's enough talk. I know you are very rich."

"Then shall we make enough oil cakes to give our neighbors?"

"Are you prepared to spend that much money?"

"Alright, my dear. Let's make enough oil cakes to share with our children then."

"Oh, why in the world do you want our children involved in this?"

Stingy Kosiya of Town Sakkara

"Then, we'll make oil cakes for the two of us."

"Why do you need oil cakes? You don't have any such craving do you?."

"Alright, my dear. I will make an oil cake just for you then."

"Excellent! That's just wonderful! But my darling, this won't be easy. If we make them here, then a lot of people will gather around us."

So, the stingy man started to think deeply. All of a sudden he jumped up with a big smile. With a clap he said:

"Yes! I've thought of a solution. Get all the ingredients required to make an oil cake, we'll go upstairs. Broken rice is more than adequate for me. Take a little water, ghee and oil. I'll be able to eat the oil cake freely there."

The nobleman and his wife took everything required to make oil cakes and started to go upstairs. Closing all doors behind them, the nobleman reached the top and breathed a sigh of relief. "Oh finally I'll be able to eat an oil cake freely."

That day, the Supreme Buddha was staying at the Jetavana Monastery in the city of Sāvatti. The Supreme Buddha addressed the Great Arahath Moggallana and said:

"Meritorious Moggallana, today Maccariya Kosiya the nobleman of the town Sakkara has locked himself on the seventh floor of his palace with the urge to eat oil cakes. He went all the way upstairs as he was scared that he might have to share them with others. You may go and tame him. Bring both of them to the city of Rajagaha using your supernatural powers. Today, these five hundred monks and I will await with interest for the oil cakes they offer as alms food."

Stingy Kosiya of Town Sakkara

Nobleman Kosiya was eagerly watching how his wife was preparing the flour for making oil cakes. Just as the oil started heating up in the frying pan, glancing through the window, they saw a visitor arrive.

Kosiya's eyes widened. His heart started to beat fast and he started to shake.

"Oh, no! This is exactly why I came all the way upstairs, to avoid people like this. Oh, it is impossible to avoid these monks. They have come here even through the sky."

With trembling lips, the nobleman spoke to Great Arahath Moggallana who was hovering in the sky:

"Oh, recluse! What are you doing hovering in the sky like this? Even if you walk in the sky, don't think that you'll get any oil cakes."

Then the Great Arahath Moggallana started to walk in the sky. "Oh! Do you think you'll be given any oil cakes because you walk like that? Listen carefully! Even if you cross your legs and sit in the sky, you won't get any oil cakes."

Then the Great Arahath Moggallana crossed his legs and sat down in the sky. "Oh, I see. So you decided to sit down as well. You are mistaken, Recluse! Even if you stand near the window you won't get any oil cakes."

Then, the Great Arahath Moggallana stood near the window.

"There's no point in you standing there. Even if you release smoke from your body, you will not get any oil cakes."

Then, Great Arahath Moggallana started to emit smoke from his body. The entire floor became covered with smoke. It irritated Kosiya's eyes. With his eyes almost shut, he stared at Great Arahath Moggallana furiously.

Stingy Kosiya of Town Sakkara

Although nobleman Kosiya felt like saying, "Even if you set this place on fire, you won't get any oil cakes," he did not say it as he feared that his palace might be damaged.

"Oh, this recluse is so greedy. It doesn't look as though he will leave unless he gets an oil cake. I must quickly give him an oil cake and get rid of him." Thinking this way, Kosiya told his wife:

"My darling, make a tiny oil cake and get rid of this recluse as soon as possible."

So his wife put a small amount of flour into the pan. But surprisingly, a huge oil cake was formed filling the whole frying pan. Nobleman Kosiya got very angry.

"Don't you understand? Who uses that much flour? Remove that oil cake from the pan and give me the spoon." With his own hands, nobleman Kosiya put a minute amount of flour into the frying pan. That gave rise to an even bigger oil cake. He removed that oil cake and put an even smaller dollop of the mixture into the pan again. Each oil cake he made turned out to be bigger than the last. Finally, the Kosiya said to his wife:

"Nothing further can be done. Give him one of those oil cakes and get rid of him."

Just as she about to take an oil cake, all the oil cakes got stuck together.

"My dear, something rather strange has happened. All the oil cakes are stuck together. They cannot be separated."

"How can that be?" snapped nobleman Kosiya. "Here, give it to me. I'll do it."

Even he was unable to separate the oil cakes. They started pulling the oil cakes in opposite directions. No matter how much they tried they could not separate them. Finally, the nobleman became very tired. He started to sweat and he felt thirsty. So he said to his wife:

"Oh, my dear wife, I don't want oil cakes anymore. You can offer them all to the recluse."

So she offered all the oil cakes to Great Arahath Moggallana. He preached the Dhamma to both of them and showed the consequences of wholesome and unwholesome actions and the results of giving alms. Both of them were captivated and inspired by the Noble Triple Gem. Nobleman Kosiya felt very happy and he changed completely.

"Oh, Venerable Sir, I did not know the consequences of giving alms before. I was happy with my miserly behaviour. But now I understand the value of giving. Oh, Venerable Sir, please take this seat and eat your meal here."

"Dear nobleman, our great teacher, the Supreme Buddha, along with five hundred other monks, is expecting these oil cakes. So I will give them right into your hands then you can offer them to the Supreme Buddha and the noble monks yourselves."

"Venerable Sir, you are saying such a strange thing. We are on the seventh floor of this palace. How can the Supreme Buddha be here?"

"Nobleman, the Supreme Buddha is dwelling at the Jetavana Monastery, which is forty five yojanas (315 miles) away from here. So, let's go there."

"Oh, Venerable Sir, how can we travel that far?"

"Nobleman, don't think too much about it. All you need to do is go all the way downstairs and step outside. The Jetavana Monastery will be right there."

Then, using his great supernatural powers, the Great Arahath Moggallana carried the palace entrance into the Jetavana Monastery. When the nobleman and his wife opened the door after going downstairs, they saw the Jetavana Monastery in front of them.

Stingy Kosiya of Town Sakkara

The two of them offered oil cakes to the Supreme Buddha and the noble monks. The oil cakes did not run out. After the monks finished eating, the two of them were also able to eat as many oil cakes as they wished.

Then they offered oil cakes to everyone else there, but still the oil cakes did not run out.

"Venerable Sir, it looks as if these oil cakes will never run out." Then, the Supreme Buddha said:

"Nobleman, in that case, put them into the pit near the Jetavana entrance."

The Nobleman put them into the pit near the entrance of the monastery. As a result, it became known as the 'oil cake burial.'

Afterwards, they listened to the Dhamma from the Supreme Buddha and became stream-entrants. They became lay disciples of the Supreme Buddha. Then they paid homage to the Supreme Buddha and went back inside the palace and returned to the town Sakkara, their home town.

From that day forward, the nobleman helped everyone with great generosity. He created ponds, lakes and gardens as well as monasteries for the community of monks. One day, a group of monks who gathered at the Dhamma Hall, had this conversation:

"Friends, the power of Great Arahath Moggallana is truly astonishing! He instantly tamed the nobleman Kosiya without undermining his confidence (in the Noble Triple Gem) or his wealth and brought them to the Jetavana Monastery. Not only that, he arranged for them to meet our great teacher, the Supreme Buddha, which gave them the opportunity to become stream-entrants. Indeed, Great Arahath Moggallana's powers are astonishing!"

Through the divine ear, the Supreme Buddha heard how Great Arahath Moggallana was being praised. Then, realizing the significance of it, the Supreme Buddha stated:

"Meritorious monks, that's exactly how a noble monk should act. Without harming the confidence or wealth of devotees or without straining their families, they must act with compassion, just like a bee that collects nectar from a flower. That is exactly how Moggallana acts." After stating this, the Supreme Buddha summarized its meaning in a Gatha and beautifully recited it.

> **Yathāpi Bhamaro Puppaṁ - Vaṅnagaṅdhaṁ Ahetayaṁ**
> **Palethi Rasamādāya - Evaṁ Gāme Munī Chare**

As a bee gathers honey from the flower without injuring its colour or fragrance, even so the sage goes on his alms-round in the village.

Meritorious children, since the bee loves honey, it goes in search of beautiful flowers. Then, without harming or impairing the flower, it brings back nectar. It does not damage the beauty of the flower and the bee is able to gather nectar. The bee gathers nectar drop by drop in order to make the honeycomb. That's how a sage-a noble bhikkhu- should behave in the village. Without distressing, cheating or deceiving lay people and without putting any pressure on them, the sage gains the four necessities. Then that sage's conduct does not harm the villagers' confidence (in the Triple Gem) or their wealth. Just like treating a wound, or like the food given to a person crossing a desert, the sage who practices the Dhamma uses the four necessities mindfully. He engages in learning Dhamma and meditation and gains the opportunity to attain fruition in the Noble path. After satisfying their basic physical needs through receiving alms, Arahaths are able to enjoy the blissful concentration of their spiritual achievements.

Many who listened to this Dhamma stanza from the Supreme Buddha benefitted immensely!

- The End -

Mahamegha English Publications

Sutta Translations
Stories of Sakka, Lord of Gods: Sakka Saṁyutta
Stories of Great Gods: Brahma Saṁyutta
Stories of Heavenly Mansions: Vimānavatthu
Stories of Ghosts: Petavatthu
The Voice of Enlightened Monks: Theragāthā

Dhamma Books
The Wise Shall Realize

Children's Picture Books
The Life of the Buddha for Children
Chaththa Manawaka
Sumana the Novice Monk
Stingy Kosiya of Town Sakkara
Kisagothami
Kali the She-Devil
Ayuwaddana Kumaraya
Sumana the Florist
Sirigutta and Garahadinna
The Banker Anāthapiṇḍika

To order, go to www.mahamevnawa.lk

www.ingramcontent.com/pod-product-compliance
Lightning Source LLC
Chambersburg PA
CBHW041235040426
42444CB00002B/170